Working for our Future
An Equal Chance for Girls and Women

Judith Anderson with Christian Aid

SEA-TO-SEA
Mankato Collingwood London

This edition first published in 2010 by
Sea-to-Sea Publications
Distributed by Black Rabbit Books
P.O. Box 3263, Mankato, Minnesota 56002

Copyright © Sea-to-Sea Publications 2010

Printed in USA

All rights reserved.

Library of Congress Cataloging-in-Publication Data

Anderson, Judith (Judith Mary)
 An equal chance for girls and women / Judith Anderson with Christian Aid.
     p. cm. -- (Working for our future)
  Includes index.
  ISBN 978-1-59771-196-8 (hardcover)
 1. Children's rights--Juvenile literature. 2. Women's rights--Juvenile literature. 3. Girls--Social conditions--Juvenile literature. 4. Women--Social conditions--Juvenile literature. 5. Sex discrimination against women. 6. Sex discrimination. I. Christian Aid. II. Title.
  HQ789.A66 2010
  323.3'52--dc22
                          2008044882

9 8 7 6 5 4 3 2

Published by arrangement with the Watts Publishing Group Ltd., London.

Editor: Jeremy Smith
Art director: Jonathan Hair
Design: Rita Storey

Produced in association with Christian Aid. Franklin Watts would like to thank Christian Aid for their help with this title, in particular for allowing permission to use the information concerning Yalda, Sri Devi, and Arlinda and Theresa which is © Christian Aid. We would also like to thank the parents of Wang Huang for the information and photographs provided.

Picture credits: Adrian Arbib/Christian Aid: 3br, 10l, 13t, 16b, 24b. Alamy: 1, 4b, 6t, 10t, 11b, 13b, 25. Annabel Davis/Christian Aid: 3bc, 6b, 7, 12t, 20-21 all. Eduardo Martino/Christian Aid: 3bl, 8-9 all, 15b, 19b, 23t. istockphoto.com: 27b.

The Millennium Development Goals

In 2000, government leaders agreed on eight goals to help build a better, fairer world in the 21st century. These goals include getting rid of extreme poverty, fighting child mortality and disease, promoting education, gender equality, and maternal health, and ensuring sustainable development.

The aim of this series is to look at the problems these goals address, show how they are being tackled at local level, and relate them to the experiences of children around the world.

Contents

Same for all?	4
Why are girls treated differently?	6
Different lives	8
The need for change	10
The Millennium Development Goals	12
Government action	14
Local solutions	16
People who help	18
Girls in school	20
Work and wages	22
Marriage and healthy families	24
Having a say	26
Action you can take	28
Glossary/Find out more	30
Index	32

The Cast

In this book follow the stories of these four children from around the world, all affected by inequality in different ways.

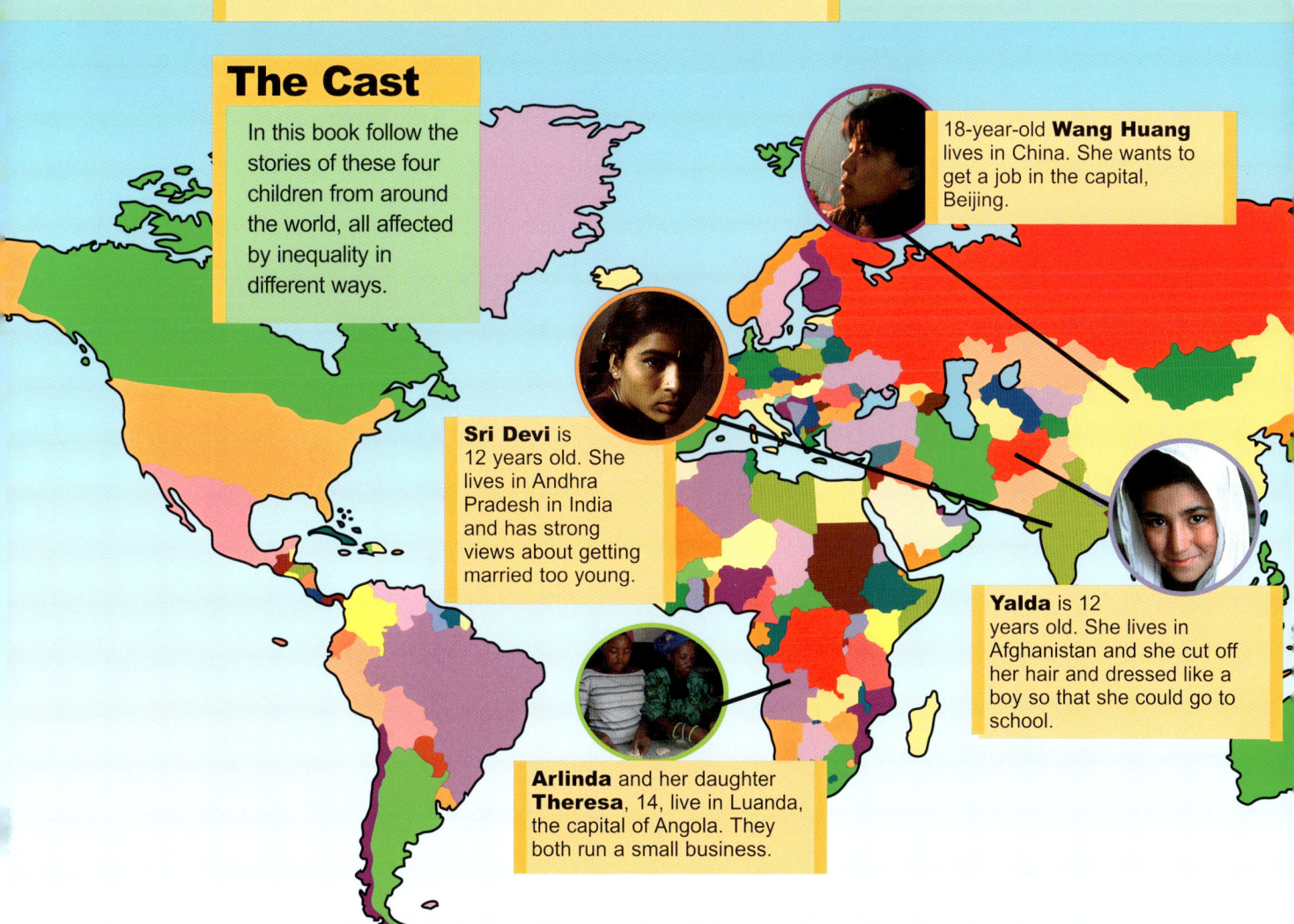

18-year-old **Wang Huang** lives in China. She wants to get a job in the capital, Beijing.

Sri Devi is 12 years old. She lives in Andhra Pradesh in India and has strong views about getting married too young.

Yalda is 12 years old. She lives in Afghanistan and she cut off her hair and dressed like a boy so that she could go to school.

Arlinda and her daughter **Theresa**, 14, live in Luanda, the capital of Angola. They both run a small business.

Same for all?

What would you like to do in the future? Maybe you would like to go to college and train to be a doctor or a teacher. You might want to be a singer or a football player. Or perhaps you see yourself running your own business or taking part in government.

Nita, age 10

" I want to work in television. I'd like to read the news. **"**

It's not fair
All children deserve the same opportunity to go to school, train for a job, and have a say in their own future. In fact, many countries have laws to make sure that every child is treated fairly and equally. Nevertheless, in some parts of the world, girls are not given the same chances as boys. This is called discrimination, and it affects girls in many different ways.

Here are a few of the things that girls are prevented from doing in some parts of the world.
- Going to school
- Driving a car
- Voting
- Choosing their own husband
- Owning property
- Running a business

No school

Not being able to go to school is one of the biggest problems facing girls in poorer parts of the world. Those who are not in school are not learning the skills they need to find a good job or stand up for themselves and demand the equal rights they deserve. While boys have the chance to build careers, girls may be forced to stay at home, carrying out tasks such as cleaning and fetching water. They may be expected to marry very young and start a family. They have little hope of building a better future for themselves.

James, age 9

“ My father is a fire officer. I want to be like him. ”

▼ A young girl collects reeds in Ethiopia instead of attending school.

? What would you like to do in the future? How would you feel if someone tried to stop you from working toward your goal?

Why are girls treated differently?

There are many different reasons why girls in some parts of the world are not given the same chances as boys. Tradition, prejudice, and fear of change all play a part. So do motherhood and family responsibilities. But the most important reason is poverty.

Too expensive to educate?

In very poor communities boys and girls still fulfill very traditional roles. In many cases it is only males who receive an education while women stay at home to help out with housework. There are many other disadvantages to being a girl in lots of developing and developed countries across the world.

Family and marriage

Because sending a child to school is expensive, girls in many countries miss out on an education. Instead, they are often expected to get married very young, so that they no longer have to be fed and clothed by their parents. Some girls from particularly poor families may even find themselves put out to work at a very young age, or made to find other ways to earn money for the family.

Families with young children or elderly or sick relatives need someone to care for them. Women generally fill this role, but such responsibility makes it more difficult for them to go out to study or to work. This problem is made worse when girls are forced to marry very young, often before they have finished their education.

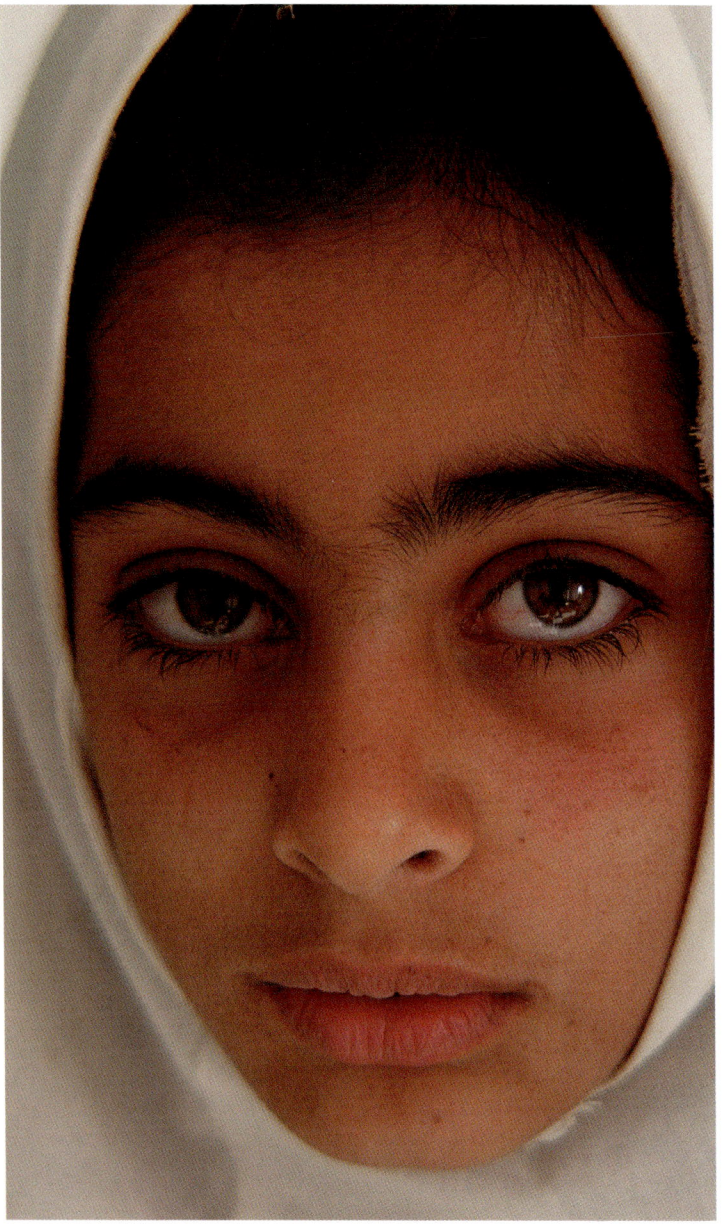

 Amina from Afghanistan is only 12 years old. Her father married her off to a man in the village for money so that he could afford to buy food for the rest of the family.

Traditional societies

In some parts of the world, women are valued less than men. Women are denied the right to an education and in some countries are not allowed to own their own property or have a say in how their community is run. Because these women have no power, it is difficult for them to change the attitudes of those around them and so the tradition of discrimination against women continues.

Discrimination in developed countries

More developed parts of the world such as the European Union have laws banning all forms of inequality between men and women. Nevertheless, some women still face discrimination. Employers may favor men over women because women are the ones who have children. Women often work part-time and sometimes find they are paid less per hour than men working full-time.

 Girls carrying out traditional "women's work" in Benin, Africa.

 All over the world, women struggle to reach the top positions, as this photo of world leaders taken at Geneva in 2003 illustrates.

? **What laws do you think could be made to prevent girls like Amina from being denied the chance to shape their own future?**

Different lives

Women and girls in some parts of the world face inequality and discrimination throughout their lives. According to the World Food Program, seven out of 10 of the world's hungry are women and girls. In developing countries, more girls than boys die before the age of five, and of the 800 million people in the world who cannot read or write, more than two-thirds are women.

Not valued

When girls are valued less than boys they are not only denied their rights to education, work, and independence—they are sometimes even denied their right to life. Girl babies may be given less food, fewer medicines, and even killed to prevent them from becoming a "burden" to their families. In some parts of the world, girls are made to feel worthless from the day they are born.

Sri Devi, age 13, lives in Andhra Pradesh in India. She belongs to the Lambada tribe, a very poor tribe that traditionally has not valued its girls as much as boys.

" When I was born, my father wanted nothing to do with me because I was not fair-skinned (he thought it would be more difficult to find a husband for a dark-skinned girl). At 10 years old I was sent out to work as a domestic worker. I spent all day washing dirty pots, pans, and dishes. **"**

Wang Huang is nearly 18 years old. She lives in Longxi, in China, and stopped going to school when her father became ill and the family had to spend nearly all their money on his treatment.

❝ I felt doomed to farm in the field all my life and marry early like the other girls in the village. ❞

Government prejudice

Prejudice isn't always the fault of families. It is sometimes forced on people by a country's leaders, or government. Yalda Shams is 12 years old and lives in Afghanistan. When the country was ruled by the Taliban government, new laws were introduced that made life very difficult for women and girls.

Yalda describes what life was like under the Taliban for women and the prejudice she suffered.

❝ Women couldn't work, like my mother, and girls couldn't go to school. I didn't go to school for six years. ❞

? **How do you think Sri Devi felt when she was sent out to work at the age of 10 by her father?**

The need for change

Equality between boys and girls, men and women is vital for many different reasons. It ensures that women and girls have the same rights to education, to jobs, to respect, and to a future. However, the benefits are felt by everyone—including boys.

> **"** All human beings are born free and equal in dignity and rights. **"**
>
> **United Nations Declaration on Human Rights**

Work and wealth

According to the Women's International Network, women do 65 percent of the world's work yet receive less than 5 percent of its income. Equal chances for girls raises families out of poverty. Learning a skill means they can earn money. This creates more wealth in the local community. There are many important jobs in teaching, engineering, and medicine that need more people. If women are allowed to fill these positions they are more likely to feel an equal part of society and speak out when they see injustice. However, it is essential that women be paid the same wage as men when they do a similar job.

▶ These women meet to sew clothes and support each other in a village near Balakot, northern Pakistan.

Health and family

Equal chances for girls means healthier families. Women who have learned to read and write are better informed about the health risks that spread disease. They tend to marry later, have fewer, healthier, better-nourished children, and are more likely to send their own children to school.

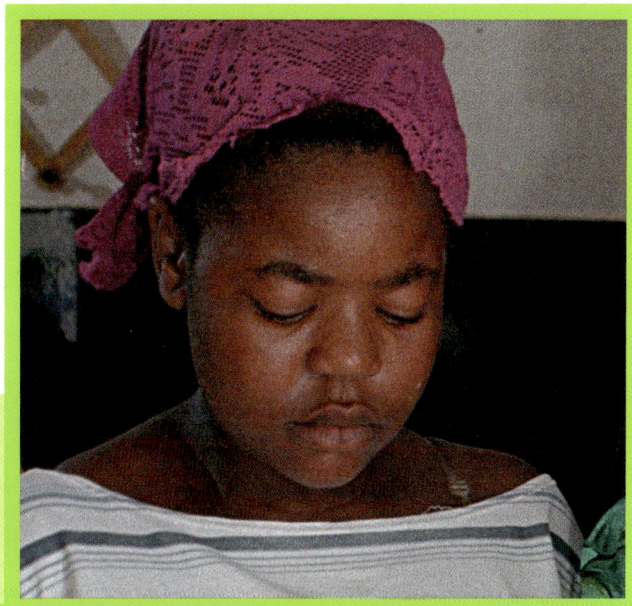

Theresa is 14 years old and lives with her mother and the rest of her family in Luanda, the capital of Angola. They fled from their home town of Bie during Angola's civil war.

❝ I couldn't go to school because of the fighting. Lots of people were dying. We had to leave. **❞**

Arlinda, Theresa's mother, found them a place to sleep on the floor of a church in Luanda. They were dependent on others to bring them food until Arlinda went to a skills center to learn about cooking and health issues.

❝ Because of the war I felt empty of knowledge. But we mothers have to find ways of taking care of everyone's life. I decided to enroll at the skills center to increase my knowledge and help my children and other children in this slum. **❞**

? In what ways do you think Arlinda's new skills might help her daughter Theresa and the other children in their community?

The Millennium Development Goals

In the year 2000 the world's leaders (above) met at the United Nations and agreed a set of eight goals that would help make the world a better, fairer place in the 21st century. Equal chances for women and girls became the third goal, though all eight goals are closely linked.

> " Gender equality is not only one of the Goals but also a means to achieve other Goals. "
>
> **Rachel Mayanja, UN special advisor on gender issues.**

The Goals

Each goal has targets that need to be achieved by a specific date, and governments have been asked to make policies to ensure these targets are met. The target for the third goal is to eliminate inequality between boys and girls in all levels of education by 2015.

THE EIGHT MILLENNIUM DEVELOPMENT GOALS

1. Get rid of extreme poverty and hunger
2. Primary education for all
3. Promote equal chances for girls and women
4. Reduce child mortality
5. Improve the health of mothers
6. Combat HIV/AIDS, malaria, and other diseases
7. Ensure environmental sustainability
8. Address the special needs of developing countries, including debt and fair trade

More boys than girls

At the moment, the number of boys enrolling in school remains far greater in many countries than the number of girls. In India, only 54 percent of girls can read and write, compared to 75 percent of boys. In very poor areas, for girls, the percentage is even lower. Countries must focus on this problem if the target of equality in education is to be met by 2015. Governments must create and support schemes to get girls to school and properly educated, such as "The Girls Forum," a scheme set up in Kenya.

> **"** When the teachers came to see me [age 12] I only knew the alphabet. **"**

After working for two years as a domestic servant, Sri Devi returned to her father's house and was sent out to work in the fields. Then one day a team of teachers came to her village to see how many children were not attending school.

Better for everyone

When a country educates both its boys and girls, it usually becomes richer, the death rates of babies and mothers usually fall, and the health and education prospects of the next generation improve. Statistics from The World Bank support these statements.

 These two teachers run "The Girl's Forum," a project to give young girls special attention in Kenyan schools.

? **Can you think of ways in which some of the other Millennium Development Goals might support the Goal of equal chances for girls and women?**

Government action

Most countries have signed up to the Millennium Development Goals. However, change cannot happen without real and determined action from governments around the world. Governments make laws, decide how money is spent, and influence the choices people have over their lives. They must use their power to make equal chances for women and girls a reality.

" It is not in the United Nations that the Millennium Development Goals will be achieved. They have to be achieved in each country by the joint efforts of the governments and the people. "

Kofi Annan, former United Nations Secretary-General

▲ A woman working in a Romanian cheese factory. Her government has introduced laws to ensure she is paid the same as a man doing the same job.

Changing laws and policies

Many women around the world are paid less than men, even when they do the same work. Governments can make this kind of discrimination illegal. Governments can also change any unfair laws about marriage and property that discriminate against women.

It is against the law for girls in India to marry before they are 18. (For boys the legal age is 21.) However, Sri Devi's father tried to give her away in marriage when she was 12.

" I would like to break out of this system where women are expected to marry early and stay at home. **"**

Education
Governments in developing countries can build more schools and training centers and make education free for all children so that parents do not have to decide whether they can afford to send their daughters to school. Richer countries can make it easier for poorer countries by canceling their debts and ensuring they have enough money to make these vital changes.

Marriage
A total of 44 countries in both the developing and developed world have laws allowing girls to marry at a younger age than boys. This is discrimination and governments should act to raise the age at which girls can marry so that it is equal to boys.

New attitudes
Many countries already have laws to end discrimination against women. However, traditional attitudes mean that often these laws are ignored. For example, each year around the world hundreds of thousands of girls are forced by their communities to marry before the legal age. Governments can do much more to inform women about their rights, promote the benefits of education for girls, and prosecute those who treat girls and women unfairly. They can also educate men to move away from "traditional" attitudes that discriminate against women.

? **What could governments do to ensure that laws against child marriage are upheld? How would this help girls like Sri Devi?**

Local solutions

Governments can change laws and invest in schools and training and health, and in businesses that benefit women and girls. However, charities and aid organizations also provide vital help by working closely with local communities to address the particular needs of women in the area where they live.

Three young girls harvest rice in Vietnam instead of attending school.

A class of Chinese girls learn at the Practical Skills Center for Rural Women.

Identify the problem

In the village where Wang Huang lives in China, school is rarely an option for older girls. Girls are not encouraged to leave and work outside of the home, because the local people believe that they will have a difficult time finding a husband. They also believe that once a girl is 20, no man will want to marry her because she is too old. As a result, girls in their teens just stay at home, waiting for a matchmaker to find them a husband.

In 1998, the Practical Skills Center for Rural Women was established to help young women like Wang Huang with writing and mathematics skills and basic training to enable them to find work in Beijing, the capital of China. It was the first organization of its kind in China, and is funded by international charities such as NetAid, as well as donations from individuals.

Find the best solution

Projects like the Practical Skills Center for Rural Women identify the specific problems faced by women and girls in their communities, and use their local knowledge to find the most appropriate solutions.

Another charity called the World Job and Food Bank works with a local partner in China to inform women about their rights. Sixty married women, all under the age of forty, went to Southwestern Petroleum Institute (SWPI) to attend a three-day training course. They learned about women's rights, women's health, and an agricultural expert gave a presentation about how to raise goats in the mountain villages.

"Our training course is completely free. We recruit students from the most deprived regions. At first we were misunderstood. People couldn't believe we were doing such a good thing. The next minute we were invited to every family and had potatoes for dinner, which was the best thing they could offer."

Ms Wu Qing, Director of the Practical Skills Center for Rural Women (logo shown above).

Sixty married women at a SWPI training session in China.

? How will the skills the women learned on the SWPI course help their community?

People who help

All sorts of people are working to improve the lives of girls and women around the world. Some are volunteers. Others are professional teachers, project managers, campaigners, and fundraisers. Many are women who have been helped themselves and now want to pass on their knowledge and skills for the benefit of the whole community.

Daw Le Le Win

When war disrupted the lives of people living in Burma (Myanmar), many fled to refugee camps over the border with Thailand. The Karen Women's Organization (KWO) was set up to work for the needs of women throughout the camps, offering advice on personal safety, teaching skills such as weaving, and speaking up for women's rights. The chairperson of the KWO in Maela camp is Daw Le Le Lin. Her name in English means "bright light."

Daw Le Le Win speaks about her aim of getting women involved in the community.

❝ We are keen to encourage women to play a role equal to that of men in the community. We have much to give, we can be strong, and, like other women around the world, be beacons of light in our community. ❞

Answering a need

Joaquina Arão is an expert in nutrition, with more than 30 years' experience. As the health education teacher at the training center in Angola attended by Arlinda and her daughter, she teaches women how to prepare economical, healthy meals with whatever ingredients are available to them. She also explains how to prevent disease through good hygiene.

> **"** We want to transmit our knowledge to the younger generation. Basically we aim to help these women protect their family and find a way of making a living. We try to open women's eyes. After they've come here, we hope that people are able to improve their lives. **"**

Joaquina shows her students how to cook economical, healthy food.

 Why do you think Daw Le Le Win and Joaquina Arao want to help women improve their lives?

Girls in school

Getting rid of inequality in education is the key target for the third Millennium Development Goal of promoting equal chances for girls and women. More girls in school is one of the best ways to reduce poverty, ensure better health for all, and provide women with an equal say in communities around the world.

Yalda speaks about how she managed to get an education.

" No one at school knew that I was a girl—I wore trousers and a cap. Not even the other boys knew! "

Yalda joins the boys

Yalda was lucky. Her father wanted her to have a good education, despite the Taliban government's view that girls should not go out to school. So, he thought of an unusual way round the problem. He suggested she cut her hair and go to school with the boys! Yalda did this for four years. Fortunately for many girls in Afghanistan, the Taliban government was overthrown in 2002 and many of the restrictions on women were lifted. There are 6,000 girls at Yalda's school now.

Yalda describes life after the Taliban.

"Before, women couldn't work, like my mother. Now it's better because we can go to school and do courses for learning. I want to be a journalist or a flight attendant when I grow up because I like to speak with people and go to other countries."

Bridge schools

Gramya is an organization working to improve the status of women in Sri Devi's region of India. When Sri Devi was picking cotton in her father's fields she was spotted by teachers from Gramya and asked to attend a residential Bridge school. Bridge schools are places where girls like Sri Devi can catch up on their studies, in preparation for regular school.

An Indian Bridge school.

"Gramya came to speak to my parents and persuade them to send me to the Bridge school. When I first came, I only knew the alphabet, but now I have reached the seventh grade. I want to qualify as a teacher."

? How do you think the lives of Yalda and Sri Devi are different from yours? How do you think they are the same?

Work and wages

Helping women into work is a big step toward independence and equality. Not only do they start to earn money, they also begin to play an important role in their communities. A woman who earns her own money, runs her own business, and perhaps employs other people can no longer be ignored by the rest of society.

Karen Hughes, U.S. Under Secretary for Public Diplomacy and Public Affairs.

" When you educate a woman, she teaches her family. Give a woman a microgrant [lend her money] so she can start a small business in her home, and she will buy shoes, milk, and books for her children with the profits. "

The lack of affordable childcare stops many women from studying or working. However, a nursery at the study center where Arlinda teaches means mothers can leave their children in safe hands.

The first step

Women need more than a new skill in order to start up a small business. They need tools and materials. In many traditional cultures, women have not been allowed to borrow money but now community banks are forming to offer poorer women a small loan, called "micro-grants," to help them buy the things they need. Once these women start to earn money from their business, they pay back the loan.

Arlinda starts her own business

Arlinda did not get a micro-grant but thanks to the education course at the IECA training center, Arlinda started making bags and baskets to sell. Soon she and her family had enough money to rent a small house. Today she also teaches crafts to other women, passing on the skills she has learned.

Arlinda shows shoppers the bags and baskets she has made.

> **"** In my family, a lot has changed. My daughters are more knowledgeable now—they know how to cook, sew, and deal with the house. They have set up a small business preparing food to order for parties and celebrations. **"**

Wang Huang looks to the future

Wang Huang also feels that her future is much brighter now that she is learning at the Practical Skills Training Center for Rural Women. She knows how difficult it is for girls from the countryside to realize their dreams.

Wang Huang reveals how how life has been changed.

> **"** I have changed greatly since I came here. The kind teachers here showed me the value of my life. I have learned to be self-confident. So I have now decided to find a good job in Beijing and send money to the Practical Skills Training Center for Rural Women. I want to help other girls like me. **"**

 Arlinda and her daughters now earn their own money. How do you think this has changed their lives?

Marriage and healthy families

When girls are taught to read and write, learn a skill, and earn a wage, they are less likely to be forced into an early marriage. Mothers who have learned about health and hygiene can take better care of their children. They are also more likely to protect themselves against disease.

Child marriage

The UN's "Declaration on the Elimination of Discrimination Against Women" states that: "Women shall have the same right as men to free choice of a spouse and to enter into marriage only with their free and full consent." It also says that "child marriage shall be prohibited." Despite this, the practice still goes on in many countries.

Girls are not only forced to marry to raise money, but marriages can also be made to settle family feuds, as was the case with Afsheen (right). When a girl gets married, she is often forced to do what the family of her husband tells her to do, and loses all her rights. There are also health problems for women who marry early. If a girl has a baby while still in her teens, her health and the health of her baby are more likely to be at risk.

Afsheen, 19, was just nine years old when she was married to a man four times her age in compensation for the murder committed by her father.

> " Since being at the Bridge school, I have gained confidence in taking a stand on early marriage. Child marriage puts an end to our education. We have children far too young. If we are not educated then we are under obligation to our in-laws and have to follow their rules. I would like to be married but not until after I have qualified as a teacher. "

Sri Devi has strong views about early marriage, especially after her father tried to give her away in marriage when she was 12 years old in exchange for a dowry of $4,500.

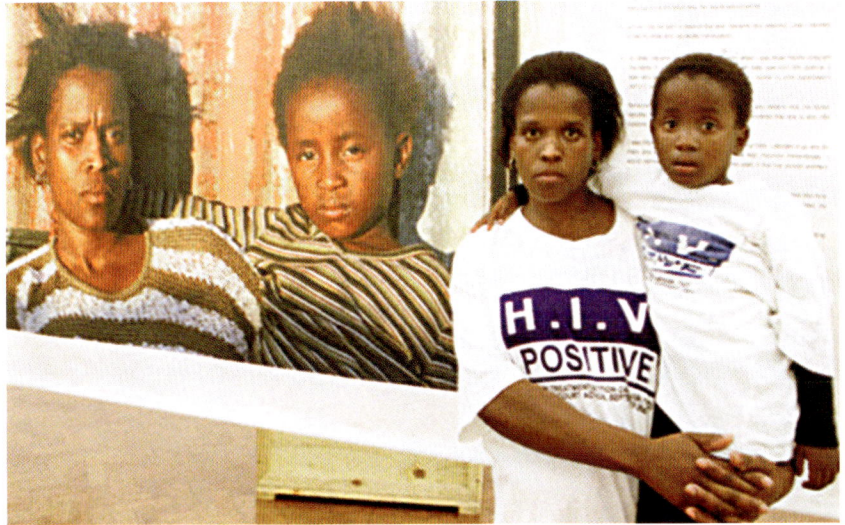

▲ This mother and son are wearing T-shirts promoting a greater knowledge of HIV/AIDS. Helping people to be aware of the problem in this way means that fewer people will be infected with the disease in the future.

Family health

Girls who go to school are more likely to learn about hygiene, contraception (planned parenthood), and healthy eating. Women who have learned to read and write are more likely to know how to protect themselves and their families from diseases like malaria and HIV/AIDS.

In Africa, children of mothers who have received at least five years of primary education are 40 percent more likely to live beyond the age of five.

? Why do you think mothers who have been to school are more likely to have healthier children?

Having a say

Giving women and girls the same chances as boys and men is not just about education, wages, and their role within the family. It is also about listening to the views of women, respecting their opinions, and giving them an equal voice in their local communities and their national governments.

Building confidence

Around the world, many women are forming self-help groups and organizations to learn from each other, support each other, and speak up for their rights in their local communities. For Arlinda, the help she received from the IECA center has meant she can now teach others in her community new skills and a way out of poverty.

Arlinda (left), inside the IECA center, explains her hopes for the future.

❝ I want to show we women are capable of doing things, and shouldn't be ashamed before a man. I would like to show women that we can be brave. ❞

Making a difference

When women take part in government, they participate in all areas of decision-making. Women have the same right as men to vote, make laws, and debate issues, such as national security, public services, crime, and foreign policy.

However, some traditional societies remain reluctant to see women in positions of leadership. In 2005 women still occupied only 16 percent of the seats in national parliaments in developed countries, and far less than that in developing countries. Fortunately, women like Moana Essa Raseta are beginning to change all of that.

▲ The Prime Minister of New Zealand, Ms. Helen Clark, arrives at NATO headquarters. She is one of the few female world leaders.

Moana Essa Raseta is the first woman governor of Ihorombe, in southeastern Madagascar. Women in Ihorombe (left) have traditionally been given a low status.

❝ Since I became governor, men have had to listen to me! When I go to a village to make a speech, everyone is there, even the women. But when it is time to discuss my speech, the women disappear and only the important men attend these discussions. So I encourage the women to meet with me separately. ❞

? Are girls and women given an equal chance where you come from?

Action you can take

Ending gender discrimination is not just a job for politicians. Everyone can get involved in making sure that girls and women get an equal chance. Speaking out on behalf of women and girls, informing people about the issues, adding your voice to campaigns, and raising money for those charities that support equal opportunities are all ways to take action and make a real difference.

▲ You could join a march for women's issues in your area.

Make people think
Hold an awareness assembly at your school to highlight some of the difficulties for women and girls around the world. Ask children to remember how it feels when something is unfair. Then tell them a story about a girl who is forced to marry young or a girl who must stay at home while her brother goes to school.

Add your voice
Do you have an opinion about the Millennium Development Goals? Have you or anyone you know been affected by any of the issues? Email your story to addyourvoice@un.org
or write to the following address:

United Nations

Cyberschoolbus

405 East 42nd Street

Rm L-170

New York, NY

10017

Challenge your government

Your government signed up to the Millennium Development Goals in 2000. But is it doing enough to make sure that the targets will be met? Write a postcard to your local representative or member of congress and ask them to explain what action they are taking to get more girls around the world into school.

Support a charity

Organize an event, such as a sponsored run or a craft sale, to raise funds for a charity that supports women and girls around the world. Larger charities, such as Christian Aid, Save the Children, and UNICEF all fund projects to help girls into school as well as campaigning vigorously for gender equality. Alternatively, research a smaller charity that you can support.

▲ Write to the leader of your country and demand that they fulfill the promises they made in 2000.

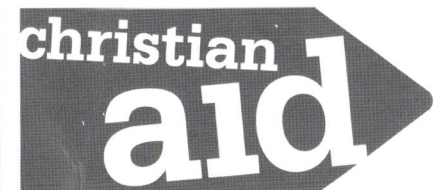 We believe in life before death

▲ The official logo of the charity Christian Aid, which helps poor children around the world, whatever their religion or sex.

? **How will you help improve the lives of girls and women like Sri Devi, Yalda, Wang Xioli, and Arlinda?**

Glossary

Charity an organization that uses money donated by members of the public to help others

Contraception preventing pregnancy

Debt money owed

Discrimination treating someone unfairly because of their sex, race, or religion

Equal rights making sure that everyone is given the same opportunities

Gender the sex of a person; male or female

Head of household the person who makes the decisions in a family

Hygiene keeping clean

Inequality unfair treatment

Micro-grant a small amount of money lent by a bank to an individual so that he or she can set up a new business

Millennium Development Goals (MDGs) Eight goals agreed by world leaders in the year 2000 with the aim of eradicating poverty and disease and promoting the rights of disadvantaged people

Mortality death

Nutrition healthy eating

Prejudice any belief or opinion that is not based on fact

Prosecute charge someone with a crime and take them to court

Refugee someone who is forced to flee their country

Status the importance or value of an individual in a community

Tradition a belief or a practice that has been upheld for a long time—often hundreds of years

Taliban Muslim group that controlled much of Afghanistan from 1995 until it was overthrown by an international military force in 2001

United Nations an organization of countries from all around the world with the aim of promoting peace, development, and human rights

Find out more

Useful websites

www.cyberschoolbus.un.org/mdgs
This site introduces all eight Millennium Development Goals with facts, photos, and video clips to illustrate each one.

Send your story or poem about how any of the issues in this book have affected you to:
addyourvoice@unorg
View stories from other children on the link above (go to "Add your voice").

www.millenniumcampaign.org/goals
Go to the above site and click on "Goal 3" to find the latest news, facts, and statistics as well as information about what you can do to help ensure an equal chance for girls and women.

www.ungei.org
The United Nations Girls' Education Initiative site has a wide range of photo stories describing a day in the life of girls from many different countries. Click on "Multimedia."

www.savethechildren.org
Go to this address and scroll down to the bar that reads "For children and teachers," then click on "children" for activities and fun ways to get involved.

www.care.org
Care says the best way to fight poverty is to invest in girls, and there is no better investment than education. Click on "Get involved" to find out what you can do to help.

Note to parents and teachers:

Every effort has been made by the Publishers to ensure that these websites are suitable for children, that they are of the highest educational value, and that they contain no inappropriate or offensive material. However, because of the nature of the Internet, it is impossible to guarantee that the contents of these sites will not be altered. We strongly advise that Internet access be supervised by a responsible adult.

Christian Aid websites

Christian Aid contributed three of the real-life stories in this book (the accounts of Sri Devi, Yalda, and Arlinda and Theresa). You can find out more about this organization by following the links below:

www.christian-aid.org.uk
The main site for the charity Christian Aid, which helps disadvantaged children and adults all over the world, regardless of their religion.

Index

action, taking 28-29
Afghanistan 6, 9, 20
Angola 11, 19, 22, 23, 26
Annan, Kofi 14

Brazil 10

charities 16, 17, 28, 29
China 8, 16, 17, 23
Christian Aid 29
Clark, Helen 27
countries,
    developing 15, 22, 27
    developed 7, 15

discrimination 4, 7, 8, 14, 15, 28

education,
    4, 6, 8, 10, 11, 12, 13, 15, 16, 18-19,
    20-21, 22, 23, 24, 25, 26
Ethiopia 5
European Union 7

government, role of 12-13, 14-15, 16, 29
groups, self-help 26
Gramya 21

health 8, 9, 11, 16, 19, 20, 24, 25
HIV/AIDS 12, 25
Hughes, Karen 22

IECA 22, 23, 26
India 9, 13, 15, 21

jobs 4, 5, 10

Karen Women's Organization 18
Kenya 13

laws 4, 7, 14-15, 16, 24

Madagascar 27
Malawi 7
marriage, child 5, 6, 15, 24, 25, 28
micro-grants 22, 23
Millenium Development Goals 12-13, 14, 20, 28, 29
Myanmar (Burma) 18

NetAid 16

organizations, aid 16

poverty 6, 8, 10, 12, 20
Practical Skills Center for Rural Women 16, 17, 23
property 4, 7, 8, 15

Raseta, Moana Essa 27
rights, basic 7, 8-9
    equal 4, 5, and throughout
Romania 14

school 4, 5, 6, 7, 8, 9, 11, 13, 15, 16, 20-21, 28
    Bridge 21, 25
society, traditional 6, 7, 9, 15, 22, 27

Taliban 9, 20, 21
teachers 4, 13, 18-19, 21, 23, 25

United Nations 10, 12, 14, 29

wage, equal 7, 10, 14, 26
work, women in 9, 10, 14, 21, 22-23
World Food Program 8
World Job and Food Bank 17